For Tammy
Keep being you!

To everyone who reads this book...
I hope you take something
important away with you.
My hope in creating this book is
that it will help you realise that
you never need to change who you
are, or what you look like.

A little tool for you to use,
to check in and see
how you're doing.

Sitting firmly at the top of the grassy hills on the previous page is the SELF-LOVE-O-METER. The SELF-LOVE-O-METER is designed for you to check in and see where you rank with love for yourself. Reaching number ten on the SELF-LOVE-O-METER means your heart is full of self-love today. Being at number one means you may just need to do a little work to get to a number that feels good for you.

At times, you may even feel that you exceed ten on the meter. You feel like your heart is full and shining with joy, which feels fantastic. However, there are also times when you may hit zero, and your heart feels like a big empty bucket. It's important to be extra gentle with yourself on these days. Remember though, if you're having a difficult time, no feeling is permanent and there are things you can do to get your SELF-LOVE-O-METER climbing again.

Over the course of the rest of the book there are little exercises that can help you to earn some hearts. These hearts are designed to help bring your SELF-LOVE-O-METER back to a point where you feel really good about yourself.

What number are you at on the SELF-LOVE-O-METER today?

Would you like to improve that number?

There are certain activities in life that really fill up your heart. It's the same with people, they can help you feel like your heart is full. Sometimes when you are around family and friends you feel secure and safe, and you know that you are appreciated and loved.

There are, of course, some people and activities which leave your SELF-LOVE-O-METER feeling empty. This can lead you to become unsure of yourself, doubt your abilities and question lots of things about yourself. It can really help to figure out what doesn't make you feel good, so that you can limit your exposure to those things.

On the next page can you think of some of the things that empty your SELF-LOVE-O-METER and some things that fill it up?

drains the tank

1.

drains the tank

2.

drains the tank

3.

fills the tank

1.

fills the tank

2.

fills the tank

3.

Sometimes we forget to check in to see if our heart is happy and full. We know when our heart is happy by the way we feel. It's an experience that we feel within the body rather than something we necessarily see on the outside.

Sometimes we see people looking happy, particularly on social media, but we don't actually know what they are experiencing inside their body. Remember happiness is a feeling. Think about the last time you felt really happy and what that felt like for you.

It's important to remember that receiving likes or hearts on social media won't bring you the same feeling on the inside, as your heart being truly full. We can get so used to relying on our appearance to receive praise, comments and likes on social media, that we forget to ask ourselves how our hearts are really feeling on the inside. The only heart that matters is the one you feel with, not the hearts online.

Imagine if we paid more attention to how full our hearts were, rather than how many hearts our selfie received on social media! Remember people can appear happy on social media, but real happiness is an experience that we feel within.

Alf

Remember

Experience is on the inside
Appearance is on the outside

Can you help Alf find his way back to his heart?

We might lose our way, but there's always a way back to our heart

Write a letter to yourself describing the things you love about yourself

Dear Me...

Don't forget to circle the amount of hearts you think you got from this exercise for your SELF-LOVE-O-METER.

Find the words

Using the letters in the grid make as many words as you can in 5 minutes. The words must be at least 3 letters long, and you can only use a letter as many times as it shown in the grid.

E	R	T
E	H	T
A	B	A

Can you find the 9 letter word? Write it in the box below.

Check In

Date: _____   S M T W T F S

Today I am learning...

_____

_____

_____

Today's
SELF-LOVE-O-METER

When my heart is full on the SELF-LOVE-O-METER it feels like...

_____

_____

_____

Rating _____

A positive experience I had was...

_____

_____

A picture of how I'm feeling

Today I am grateful for...

_____

_____

_____

So, what is body image?

You might think that body image is about what you see in the mirror. In many ways it is, but it involves so much more than just your reflection. Any image you see is initially viewed with your eyes. It is then put through the big processor that is your brain. After it goes to your brain, you will have thoughts about what you have seen. You will also have feelings about what you have observed, and often act in a particular way as a result of that. Therefore, body image has 4 components which are listed below.

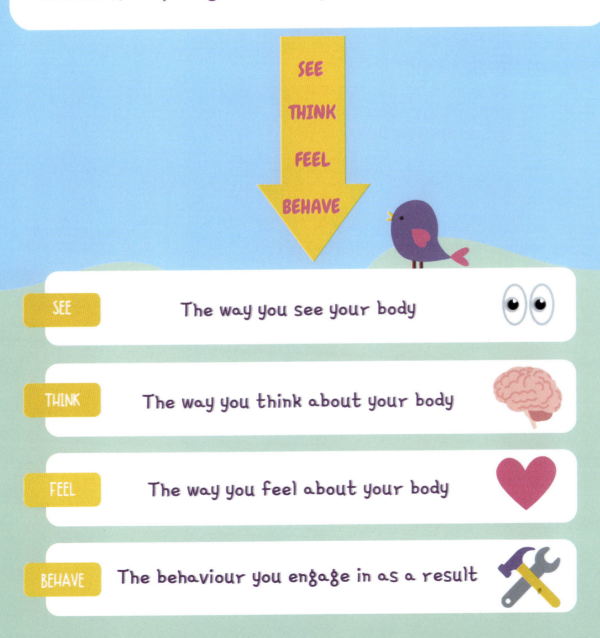

SEE	The way you see your body
THINK	The way you think about your body
FEEL	The way you feel about your body
BEHAVE	The behaviour you engage in as a result

Body image is not only about what you see with your eyes. Body image is a body experience. Body image involves your thoughts and feelings about what you see in the mirror.

Having a healthy body image goes beyond what you see reflected in the mirror. Having healthy body image means being able to manage your thoughts and feelings about what you see in the mirror.

Body image is the picture you create of yourself. However, the picture you see may not be exactly how you look. This picture can be easily influenced.

Very often the picture you have of yourself changes. These changes might be because you are not in a good mood. You might be experiencing negative thoughts, or you might feel under pressure to keep up with others.

Alf needs help with his body image

Alf is in a really bad mood today. He is feeling very angry and frustrated. Alf happens to look in the mirror while being in a bad mood. He finds it really difficult not to have negative thoughts about himself. He is finding it challenging to see himself clearly. Can you help? draw a line from Alf to the mirror that contains a reflection of Alf.

Sometimes what we see is not our physical reflection. Sometimes we see a reflection of how we are feeling.

Let's take a look at...
What you see

What you see in the mirror is just a reflection of your physical self. The mirror is just a piece of glass that contains an image of you. The image that appears in the mirror is not a problem, but sometimes because of what happens next, it can cause problems.

The image you see is then processed by your brain, and you start having thoughts and feelings about your reflection.

Let's address...
What you think

You have your own unique thoughts, but you may also have thoughts that are not necessarily developed by yourself. You might have thoughts that are influenced by other people's beliefs, opinions and values.

The thoughts you have about your body are often influenced by your friends, family and what you see on TV and social media. Some people will have very positive thoughts about themselves and their bodies, other people may have more negative thoughts. It's not your body that causes problems but, your thoughts about your body.

The brain is an amazing organ that is in charge of everything that you do. The brain is where your thoughts are formed. Sometimes these thoughts are not as nice as you would like them to be. The amazing thing is that you have the power to change these thoughts.

If a TV show came on that you really didn't like, would you keep watching it? I bet you would change the channel. Your thoughts can sometimes be like TV shows that you don't like, and you may need to change the channel from time to time. The great news is you have the remote control.

Your thoughts are not real. Your thoughts are just ideas that your mind has presented to you due to your surroundings. Your thoughts are as real as you make them. The more attention you give to a thought, the bigger and more complex that thought becomes. Remember...what you focus on, grows.

Did you know?

Your brain is a massive processor that processes about 70,000 thoughts each day.

Can you decode the secret message? Use the key to break the code

Secret Message: _____

Managing your thoughts toolbox

Over the next few pages you will find some of the thoughts exercises that are in Alf's thoughts toolbox. These are Alf's favourite exercises for managing unhelpful or unwanted thoughts. He takes these out of his toolbox whenever he needs to, and you can try one, or all of these exercises the next time you have unwanted or unhelpful thoughts. There is no particular exercise that's better than the other. Pick the one that you feel is right for you, the one that brings you the most relief. Use it as many times as you need.

You may find that on particularly challenging days you need to use two, or maybe all of these exercises and that's absolutely OK. Sometimes your brain can be a little stubborn, and you may need to try things a few times before you see any results.

Remember that thoughts are not permanent. They are not necessarily true. Unhelpful thoughts will eventually pass.

Use the tools below as required

Letting go of your thoughts

What are some anxious thoughts that you might need to let go of? Write them down on the balloons below and visualise letting the balloons go, floating way up high.

Let those unhelpful thoughts go.

Stopping your thoughts

Sometimes when you think of something negative and proceed to keep thinking about it, the thought becomes stronger. Just because a thought comes into your mind does not make it true. Just because a thought comes into your mind doesn't mean that you need to give it attention. Try putting an imaginary stop sign in front of the thoughts that you don't like.

Changing your thoughts

If a negative thought comes to mind, you can change it by looking at the bigger picture. Not everything you think is true and often you only take a very small part of information to formulate your beliefs. Try looking for all of the information before formulating a belief.

NEGATIVE TO POSITIVE

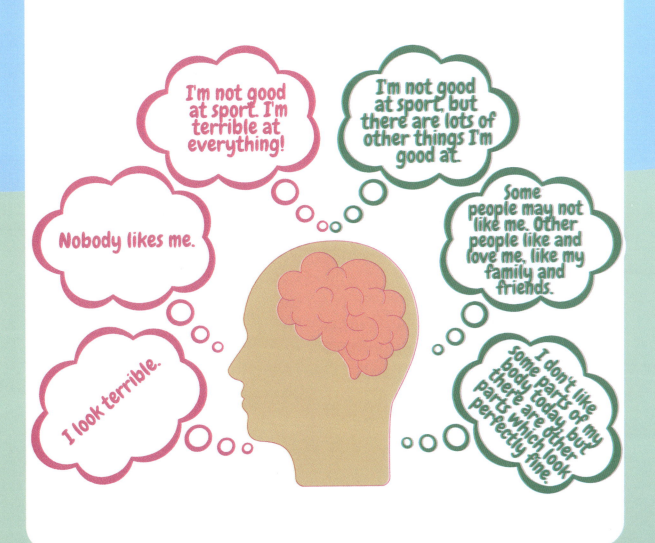

- I'm not good at sport. I'm terrible at everything!
- Nobody likes me.
- I look terrible.
- I'm not good at sport, but there are lots of other things I'm good at.
- Some people may not like me. Other people like and love me, like my family and friends.
- I don't like some parts of my body today, but there are other parts which look perfectly fine.

Getting out of your head!

You can spend a lot of time living in your head, thinking about the various problems and challenges in life. When you don't like how your head is thinking, you have a choice to leave the head and come back into the body. You can try this by simply putting your hand on your heart and putting all of your energy into feeling the beats. You can also slow down your breathing and really focus on the inhales and the exhales.

Bring all of your attention to your heart beating. Feel the rhythm of your heart beating. Feel the strength of your heart beating. Concentrate all of your energy on your heart. Pumping in beautiful rhythm, powerfully, loudly.
What does it feel like?

Bring all of your attention to your breathing. Take a deep inhale through the nose and exhale slowly and deeply through the mouth. Feel the air fill your lungs as you inhale. Feel your lungs empty as you exhale. Repeat this pattern, keeping all of your attention on your breath.
What does it feel like?

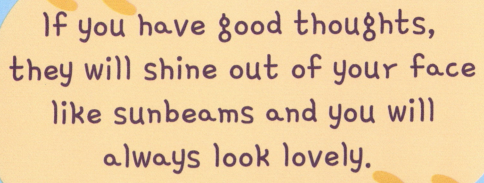

"If you have good thoughts, they will shine out of your face like sunbeams and you will always look lovely.

Roald Dahl"

Check In

Date: _____   S M T W T F S

Today I am learning...

_____
_____
_____

Today's
SELF-LOVE-O-METER

Rating _____

A picture of my thoughts

Favourite thoughts exercise

_____
_____
_____

A positive thought I have is...

_____
_____

Today I am grateful for...

_____
_____

Let's examine...
How you feel

When you think negative thoughts you tend to experience negative feelings, or feelings that you don't like.

When you have certain feelings, they can really weigh you down, or make you feel very heavy. You will feel that heaviness in your body. Feeling heavy feelings does not mean you are heavy. It means that you have a feeling that weighs a lot.

When you think negative thoughts, you will feel heavy feelings.

When you think positive thoughts, you will feel lighter feelings.

Heavy or light feelings

Think of the last time you experienced any of the feelings below. How did it feel in your body? Was it heavy like a brick in your body, or light like a balloon. Tick the appropriate box below.

	Heavy ♥	Light ♥
Happy	☐	☐
Sad	☐	☐
Lonely	☐	☐
Nervous	☐	☐
Excited	☐	☐
Angry	☐	☐
Tired	☐	☐
Proud	☐	☐
Anxious	☐	☐

Exploring your feelings

How do you feel when it's your birthday?

How do you feel when it rains?

How do you feel when someone hugs you?

How do you feel when you have a bad dream?

How do you feel right now?

We all have feelings. Some feelings we prefer to others. Experiencing happiness is far more favourable than experiencing sadness. However, there are no bad feelings. All feelings are very valid and feelings are just a part of what it means to be human.

Certain feelings can be experienced as being heavier than others. We can feel things at various degrees of intensity. For example we may feel slightly sad and it feels a little heavy, but we can manage. However, we might feel extremely sad at times, and this can be quite difficult for us to carry. This is where we might need to ask for some help from an adult, to help us cope with our feelings.

Feelings are experiences within our bodies. Feelings occur in different parts of our body. For example, some people feel anger in their stomach, fists, or head, while others experience sadness in their chest or heart space. We are all unique, so we embody feelings in our own individual way. It's important to get to know how you uniquely embody feelings. This knowledge can make it less scary when we experience strong feelings. Rather than something to be 'fixed', feelings become information about a need that longs to be met. For example, we may need to cry, talk with somebody, or express our anger. One of the greatest fears we can have is a fear of the unknown. Therefore, it makes sense to get to know your feelings.

There are some feelings which we can find really challenging, but remember feelings will pass.

Draw where you feel

Draw arrows to the different parts of your body where you experience the various feelings.

Draw how you feel

Drawing arrows to the different parts of your body when you are experiencing different feelings can be really helpful. It helps you to identify how and where you feel these emotions. When feelings become very familiar to you, you feel safer with them. It also can help you to explain to an adult what is going on for you.

There are certain parts of your body where you experience feelings more than others. Recognising this helps you to distinguish the feeling from the body part. For example, if you experience anger in your stomach, your stomach may not feel good. It doesn't mean that there is anything wrong with your stomach, you may just have a stomach full of feelings or emotions.

Now that you have identified where you experience the feelings in your body, can you explain how they feel? Is the feeling heavy or light? Does it have a colour? Does it have a sensation. Does it move or is it stationary? Is it solid or empty? Draw or write the answers in the box below.

Find the feelings hidden in the grid

BORED　　**JOYFUL**　　**CONFUSED**　　**SAD**

ANGRY　　**SCARED**　　**SURPRISED**　　**CALM**

HAPPY　　**WORRIED**　　**NERVOUS**　　**TIRED**

Managing your Emotional Energy

Your feelings will eventually pass, just as the clouds also pass. It's OK that you experience less favourable feelings at times. However, there are a few things you can do to support yourself, if your feelings are exceptionally strong. These exercises help to calm your nervous system down, and can be particularly helpful during times of stress, anxiety and feeling overwhelmed.

These exercises can be a really useful tool to help you to relax. You don't have to be experiencing strong feelings to use these. The exercises can be used as a form of self-care. You can put a lot of attention into taking care of your physical appearance, but it's also really important to take care of your well-being too.
On the following few pages, Alf has listed some of his favourite self-care exercises.

5-4-3-2-1
Grounding Technique

This grounding technique can really help if you are experiencing feelings that are very strong or overwhelming.

 Find **5** things you can **see**

 Find **4** things you can **touch**

 Find **3** things you can **hear**

 Find **2** things you can **smell**

 Find **1** thing you can **taste**

Square Breathing

Start at the top left of the square. Trace your finger to the right while you take a deep breath in. Hold your breath for four seconds as you trace the second side. Breathe out as you slide left. Hold your breath for four seconds, as you trace back up the square.

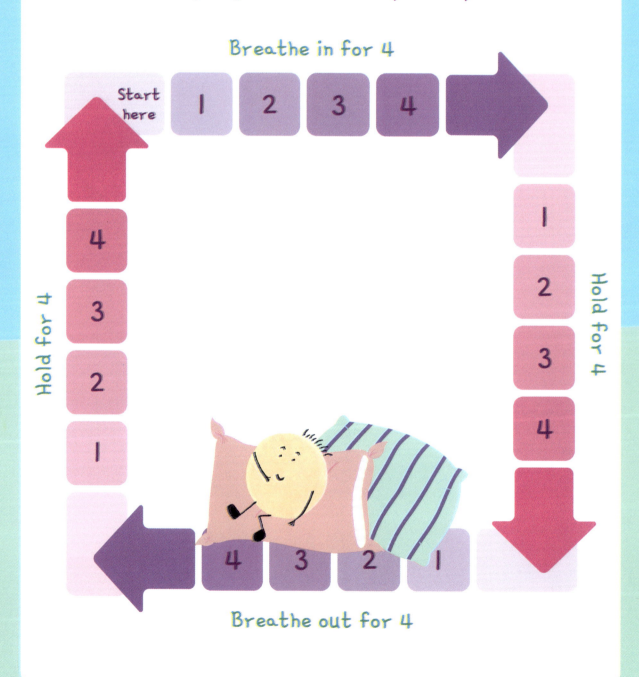

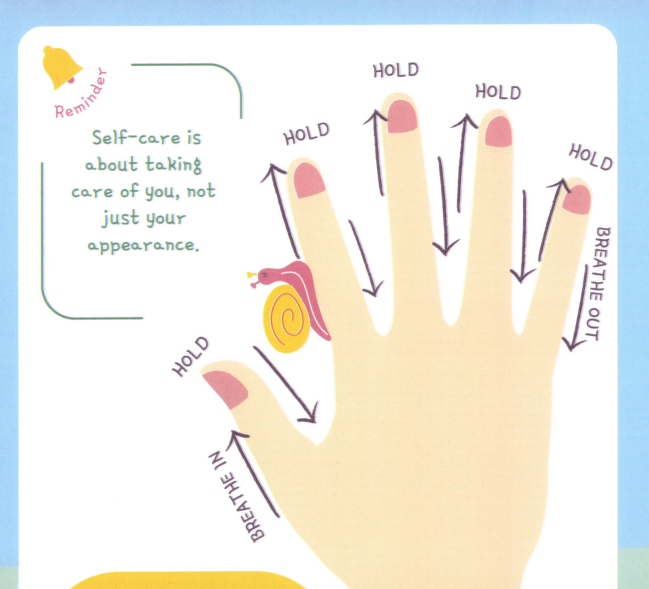

Releasing Emotional Energy

We often judge emotions as negative or positive. Try not to judge how you feel. All emotions are valid and are neither good nor bad.

Emotions are energy in the body. The emotional energy needs to be released. If you're feeling sad, you may feel the need to cry. It's so important that you let your body do what it needs to do. It's never good to stuff your emotions down. Stuffing your emotions down is like putting them in a bottle. Over time there will be too much and the bottle will potentially overflow or explode. You won't explode like a bottle but your emotions might explode out of you.

Your body looks for a way of releasing emotion. If you bottle up your emotions, it can cause you to suffer much more in the long-term. Your emotions become far stronger and far more difficult to experience. If you need to cry, then cry, and remember that no feeling lasts forever.

WARNING
Do not store emotions in here. Feel them to release them.

Check In

Date: _____   S M T W T F S

Today I am learning...

_____
_____
_____

Today's
SELF-LOVE-O-METER

Rating _____

**A picture of
my emotions**

**Favourite emotions
exercise**

_____
_____
_____

**A positive emotion
I have is...**

_____
_____
_____

**Today I am
grateful for...**

_____
_____

Last but not least...
How you behave

Sometimes, when you look in the mirror, you might have thoughts and feelings about your body that you don't like. You may be unsure how to handle these thoughts and feelings. You might sometimes be led to believe that changing your outside appearance will fix your inner experience.

The reality is, if you are unhappy, then something does need to change, but it's not yourself, or your body. You often need to change how you are thinking or feeling about your body. It helps to question what you are being told by television and social media.

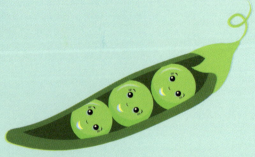

Changing your outside appearance won't change the feeling on the inside. It's a bit like having a house that's really messy inside. You might really want the house to look better, so you paint the outside of the house. Painting the outside will make the outside of the house look different, but nothing will change on the inside. The mess will still be there.

If you want things to change on the inside, you must address these inner issues. Similarly, when it comes to your feelings, the work you do to feel better requires an inside-out approach. If you fix the inside, everything feels better. The more comfortable you are on the inside, the more comfortable you will feel about the outside.

When you start changing your appearance in search of happiness, you can often make things worse. Poor Alf still looks unhappy, and he also has no money left after spending it all on paint. He is still unhappy and now he is poor!

Relying on your appearance to make you happy means constantly needing to change yourself as fashion trends come and go. This disconnects you from your true self. You begin to rely on the outside world to tell you what will make you happy, instead of listening to your own heart.

Can you help Alf find his way back to his true self?

Try telling yourself daily that you're OK just as you are. Remind yourself that there's absolutely nothing that you need to change about yourself.

Don't forget to circle the amount of hearts you think you got from this exercise for your SELF-LOVE-O-METER.

Enhancing your Body Image

Over the last number of pages, we have looked at the different components of body image. We have identified that what we see in the mirror is heavily influenced by our thoughts and feelings. It's important to take care of our thoughts and feelings around our body. Hopefully you will have found some of the exercises helpful.

♥

We only have one body, and it's important that we treat it with respect. We can show our body kindness with the words we use, and also the actions that we take. Over the next few pages, we will be looking at some of the ways that we can develop a better relationship with our body.
How does your body feel right now?
What do you think it might need?

Your body is your home.
Take good care of it.

Write a letter to your body, thanking it for all that it does for you

Dear Body...

Don't forget to circle the amount of hearts you think you got from this exercise for your SELF-LOVE-O-METER.

Screen Time

It's widely known that we have far too much screen time.

Too much time on screens can negatively affect our well-being.

It is so much better for our health to go outside and connect with our friends.

We have a lot of information coming from social media which isn't always helpful.

Listen to the Silence

It can be really hard trying to juggle all of the expectations from social media. Sometimes it can be useful to just power off.

If you are on social media, it's a really good idea to take regular breaks. Spending time with your friends in person, getting out into nature, being creative and pursuing hobbies will make you feel much better than scrolling ever will.

When you disconnect from social media ...

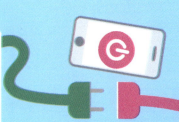

...you reconnect with yourself, your hobbies and the people who bring you joy.

Did you know?

Being outside helps increase serotonin levels. Serotonin is a chemical which helps boost your mood.

Imagine if we spent as much time charging our heart, as we did charging our phone.

Affirmations

Have you ever heard of an affirmation? An affirmation is a positive statement that people repeat to themselves. An affirmation can help you to change unhelpful thoughts that you might have about yourself, to more helpful ones. Not only are you changing your thoughts, but you are also strengthening the thoughts you want your mind to think.

"I'm good enough as I am" is an example of a positive affirmation. When you believe good things about yourself, you feel good. When you say negative things about yourself you are also affirming a statement to yourself that you may end up beginning to believe. How do you think you might feel if you end up believing negative statements about yourself? You literally can change your thoughts and your mood. How powerful is that? That sounds like a superpower to me!

Could you try telling yourself one or two affirmations every morning when you wake up, or before you go to sleep at night?

Did you know? You can change the structure of your brain by changing your thoughts, this is called neuroplasticity.

Alf's affirmation suggestions

- I am loved no matter what I look like.
- My heart is what makes me beautiful.
- My worth is not determined by my appearance or the amount of likes on social media.
- I am enough as I am.
- My body is a gift.

Decode the secret message

Look at the pictures below, and then write the names of each picture in numerical order to complete the crossword, and decipher the secret message.

Don't forget to circle the amount of hearts you think you got from this exercise for your SELF-LOVE-O-METER.

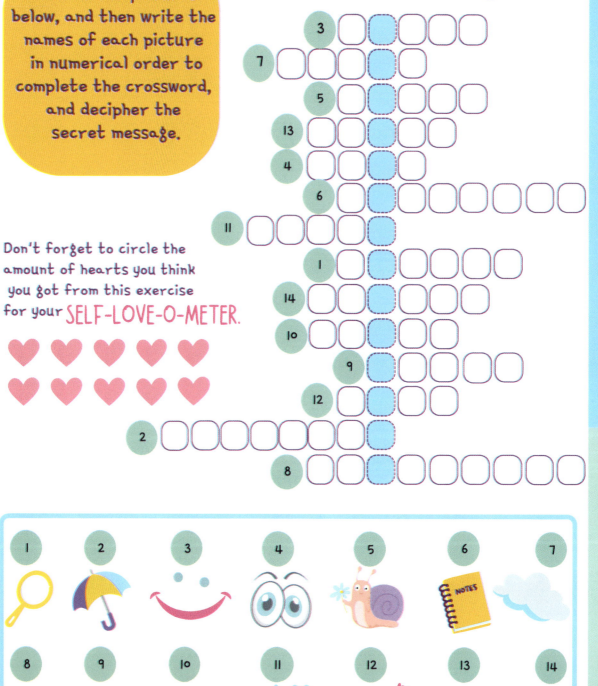

Secret Message: _____

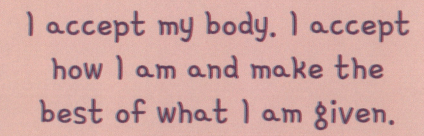

"I accept my body. I accept how I am and make the best of what I am given.
Kate Winslet"

Check In

Date: _____   S M T W T F S

Today I'm grateful for
_____
_____
_____

Today's
SELF-LOVE-O-METER

Rating

A picture of
how I'm feeling

Today's
affirmation
_____
_____
_____

Things I like about
myself today
_____
_____
_____

Things I like about
my body today
_____
_____
_____

My Body, My Friend

Your body is simply amazing. There is so much going on with your body that you can see, and loads you can't see. It works extremely hard to look after you and keep you well. Can you find some of the words that relate to your body?

```
C F F W T B E U F H H K U Q K T
B H D W Z N N X A K J Z I W W N
P U P U M E E E S E V B J D P E
H A O B E B R G C D R C X P U I
P X I G E L G D I K S J N N X L
S O B P Y N E M N L Q H I X F I
J T W S I T T C A E L Q V U V S
V J R L V G I G T C U E A E Z E
Q V A O L I C Q I E N S T H E R
T E S R N S M U N A E G X N A D
H J L Z D G R A G G I V R X I H
L U E R E O O P F L E X I E E F
H A R D W O R K I N G A H T W R
U M N D D Y E L B A P A C C C X
T A N V Q A A D A P T I V E L A
X K G N I T S E R E T N I M D K
```

STRONG   **RESILIENT**   **HARDWORKING**

FASCINATING   **HEALING**   **INTERESTING**

UNIQUE   **ENERGETIC**   **ACTIVE**

INTELLIGENT   **CAPABLE**   **ADAPTIVE**

Comparing

When we compare ourselves to others, we often compare their best features against what we think are our worst features. This doesn't sound like a fair comparison. When we compare ourselves, we are bound to feel sad and uncomfortable. We often think so much about others that we forget to value ourselves and our own unique qualities. Remember that everyone is amazing, and that means that you are amazing too.

Body Positivity

Can you think of some things you like about your body? Write them down on a piece of paper and put them into an empty jar. Each time you think of something nice, write it down and put it into the jar. You can add to this as many times as you like.

Open up your jar when you're not feeling too great about your body. Take out some of the pieces of paper. Read as many nice things as you need to. Remind yourself that how you're thinking now, and how you're feeling now is temporary. You didn't feel the same way when you wrote down these things.

Don't forget to show yourself some love. How many hearts did you earn today for your SELF-LOVE-O-METER?

Big Jar of Positive Body Image

You can decorate your jar any way you like. However, it doesn't matter how it looks. Remember, it's what's on the inside that counts.

In the picture frame below draw a picture of yourself. Label the parts of yourself you appreciate, along with why you love them.

Body Respect

There's a lot of discussion around body and health, and sometimes the mixed messages can be confusing. There's an abundance of information about how to be healthier and what it means to be healthy. However, the problem with this information is that we may end up following a set of rules without listening to our bodies. Our bodies are constantly giving us information about what they need, whether it's sleep, rest, food or water. When we ignore these needs, our bodies won't be very happy.

There are certain messages out there that tell you that to be happy, you must look a certain way. In reality, happiness comes from within. There will be some days when you don't love everything about your body, but on those days, try to at least like it. Similarly, there will be days when you don't love everything about the people around you, but you can still show them respect.

On the days when you don't feel as good in your body as you want to, try remembering all of the amazing things that your body does for you. Every day it's working hard to keep you well. It's important that you work with your body, and not against it. A nice way of showing respect to your body is to thank it for all that it does and treat it with kindness

Alf's Body Respect Suggestions

Listen to your hunger and full signals.

Wear clothes that are comfortable and fit your body.

Treat your body with kindness and love.

Do nice things for your body, like having a bath, relaxing, meditating, taking deep breaths, or reading a book.

Stop comparing yourself to others.

Remember that we all come in different shapes and sizes.

Remember happiness is not the size of your body, it's the size of the smile on your face.

Pay your body a compliment.

Which of these will you try? How many hearts do you think you would get for this exercise for your SELF-LOVE-O-METER.

Self-Esteem

When we are young, we are born with intact self-esteem. It could be compared to being like a lovely yellow slice of cheese, that's solid, strong and complete.

Over the years, we start getting messages from TV, social media, and people around us telling us that we are not good enough. We sometimes start believing that we are not enough as we are, and that we don't look as good as we should. Each time we believe those messages or say unkind things about ourselves, we are creating holes in our self-esteem. When we don't have good self-esteem, it can make us feel very sad.

If you notice that your self-esteem is low, try giving yourself some compliments. Remember that every nice thing you say about yourself is helping your cheese slice to be intact again. Each unkind thing you say puts a hole in the cheese.

Take one if needed but remember, you need to compliment yourself first.

Help Alf to find some pieces of his self-esteem. When he reaches the centre he can collect the missing pieces. He will need to collect the compliments in order to get the cheese.

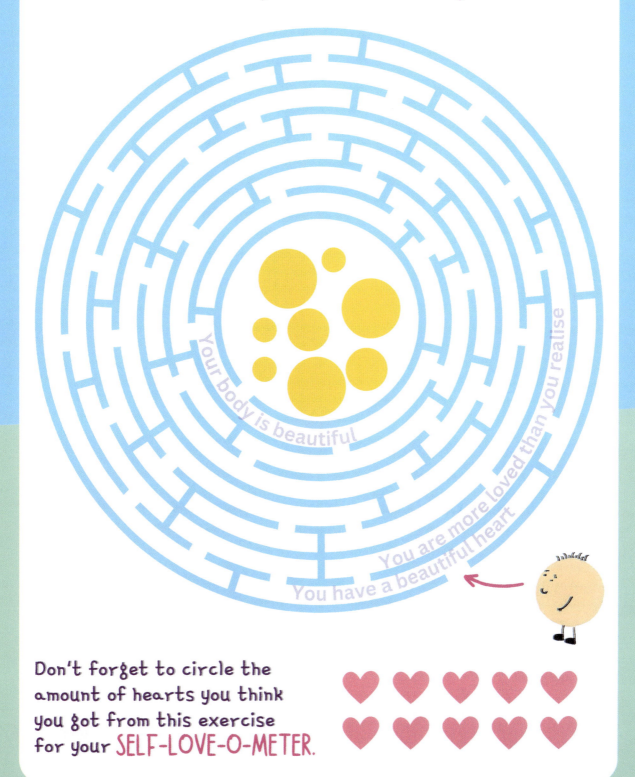

Don't forget to circle the amount of hearts you think you got from this exercise for your SELF-LOVE-O-METER.

Self-Esteem Jars

Self-esteem, as described in the dictionary is "having confidence in one's own worth or abilities".
There are many ways for a person to assess their self-esteem as a human being. Some of these ways are more helpful than others.

Some people can put a lot of value into their appearance, which can create quite a few problems.
When you put all of your worth or value on your physical appearance, it's almost like putting everything you are into one jar. You are depending on that one jar for your entire happiness.

Problems can occur when you put all parts of your self-esteem into one jar. If that jar breaks, you have no self-esteem left, and you won't feel very happy.

It's so much better to divide your self-esteem between different jars. If something happens to one jar, it won't end up being a disaster, as you have other jars to rely on.

You have reached the end of this book.
Thank you for taking the time to read it,
and I truly hope that you have enjoyed it.
As you reflect on what you have read,
I would like to remind you that body image
is so much more than what you
see in the mirror.

You are **more** than what you see in the mirror.

Love,
Alf

Printed in Great Britain
by Amazon